rst Printing, 2008
cond Printing, 2010

lished by THE INSTITUTE FOR BYZANTINE
MODERN GREEK STUDIES, INC.
Gilbert Road
ont, Massachusetts 02478-2200

y of Congress Control Number: 2003113210

d in the United States of America

ound ISBN 1-884729-73-8
ound ISBN 1-884729-74-6

SACRED CATECHISM OF THE ORTHODOX CHURCH

CHRIST THE TEACHER

Byzantine icon, second half of XVth century. On the Book of the Gospels which Christ holds is writen:

"Come unto me, all ye that labor and are heavy laden, and I will give you rest. Take my yoke upon you, and learn of me" (Matthew 11:28-29).

SACRED CATECHISM OF THE ORTHODOX CH

By

DEMETRIOS N. VERNAR

Translated from the original
CLAUDE DELAVAL CC
M.A., University College

Edited and augmen
CONSTANTINE C
Ph.D., Harv

INSTITUTE FO
AND MODERN
115 Gi
Belmont, Mass

Fi
Se
Al
Co
Pub
AND
115
Beln

Libra

Printe

Clothb
Paperb

PREFACE[1]

By

BERESFORD POTTER

Cobham's translation of this Catechism of the Greek Orthodox Church will be welcome to many English-language readers.

Being approved by the Patriarch and Synod of Constantinople, it may be regarded as an authoritative statement of the teaching of the Eastern Orthodox Church at the present day.

God is spoken of as the infinite Creator and Upholder of all things. Man is spoken of as having Divine qualities, but in a lower measure and degree. Christ's work is described as mainly to save man.

On the questions of Confession before participation in Holy Communion, of the true meaning of fasting which is described as "cleansing the soul from evil thoughts and desires and sin," and on the

[1] Abridged.

proper observation of Sunday, viz., "devoting the whole day to God," there is much from which we may derive benefit.

The perpetual Virginity of the Blessed Virgin Mary is plainly taught.

The priest's power to forgive sins is distinctly laid down. As regards the Rule of Faith, Scripture, Tradition, and the decisions of the Seven Oecumenical Synods are relied on. Christ's promise to His disciples of the Comforter [The Holy Spirit] is interpreted as applying to the decisions of these Synods. Our Lord's Divinity is strongly insisted on, so is the doctrine of the Holy Trinity.

BERESFORD POTTER
Archdeacon in Cyprus

Nicosia, Cyprus
December, 1902

PREFACE
By
CONSTANTINE CAVARNOS

While doing research in the field of Orthodox theology at Harvard College Library (Widener) some years ago I discovered a book entitled *A Catechism*, by D. N. Bernardakis (Demetrios N. Vernardakis), translated by an Englishmen named Claude Delaval Cobham, Commissioner of Larnaca, Cyprus, and a graduate of University College, Oxford. It was published in 1903 at Nicosia, Cyprus, which at that time was under British dominion, with a Preface by another Englishman, "the Venerable Beresford Potter, M.A., Archdeacon in Cyprus."

The book was probably published for the information of the British officials of the island of Cyprus, to help them better understand the religion of their Greek subjects, who constituted by far the greater part of the population of the island. It is very likely that the publication of this book was also prompted by the lively discussions at that time among English churchmen regarding the possibility of the union of the Church of England with the Orthodox Church. Some of these churchmen corresponded with prominent Greek theologians. A book such as Vernardakis' Catechism would have been a very valuable resource in this matter, in view of the fact that the original of which it is a translation has the official endorsement of the Patriarch and the Synod of Constantinople.

Going carefully over the English-language version I found the text very concise, precise, clear, analytical, extremely edifying, truly Orthodox in substance and in the manner of presentation.

Lately, seeing the great need for such a book, I decided to publish it, after comparing it with the original, Greek edition. I found that Harvard Library does not have a copy of it. Upon investigation, I discovered that the only library in the United States that has a copy of the Greek edition is that of the University of Cincinnati, but that it does not circulate. However, at my entreaty, the Librarian sent me photocopies of some pages that I thought would be especially helpful.

From these, I learned that in December of 1869, the Patriarchate of Constantinople announced a competition for the best Catechism, to be used in the Greek schools of Constantinople. This city had at that time a Greek population of several hundred thousand. The selection was to be made a year later. Vernardakis wrote and submitted a book, entitled Ἱερὰ Κατήχησις, "Sacred Catechism." It was selected as the best one.

In 1874, a second, definitive edition of his *Sacred Catechism* was published at Constantinople, by the Printing House A. Koromelas. This edition includes a formal statement about it by Patriarch Anthimos of Constantinople, dated June 2, 1872, and a Foreword by him, accompanied by the names of the ten members of the Holy Synod. There follow Vernardakis' Preface to the First edition of his book, his Introduction to the new edition, and the teachings of the Orthodox Church as set forth by him, divided into three Parts. PART ONE (ΜΕΡΟΣ ΠΡΩΤΟΝ) is listed as DOCTRINAL (ΔΟΓΜΑΤΙΚΟΝ); PART TWO (ΜΕΡΟΣ ΔΕΥΤΕΡΟΝ), as CEREMONIAL (ΙΕΡΟΤΕΛΕΣΤΙΚΟΝ); and PART THREE (ΜΕΡΟΣ ΤΡΙΤΟΝ), as ETHICAL (ΗΘΙΚΟΝ).

In his Foreword, Patriarch Anthimos states that the Ecclesiastical Committee which was appointed to select the best among the Catechisms that had been submitted in response to the contest that was announced by the Patriarchate of Constantinople in December of 1769, after very careful and detailed examination of the submitted works selected the book *Sacred Catechism* of Vernardakis as the best of all in existence. This decision, adds Anthimos, was validated by himself and by the Most Holy Synod of Constantinople. The same Committee, he says, chose another book by Vernardakis, his *Sacred History*, as likewise the best work on this subject. Finally, he says that both these works of Vernardakis have been recommended by him and the Holy Synod to be adopted by the Greek schools of Constantinople for the instruction of Orthodox youth.

The 1874 edition is comprised of 256 pages, whereas the English-language edition has only 37. The brevity of the latter is due to the much smaller font used, the great number of lines per page, and the omission of the already mentioned texts of the Patriarchate, of Vernardakis' Preface and Introduction, and of his innumerable footnotes, which are intended for the teachers of the Catechism. The brevity of the English edition does not seriously affect its usefulness for (a) teaching young people the essentials of the Orthodox Faith, and (b) for acquainting adults of other Faiths with the essence of Orthodoxy—especially persons who are considering becoming members of the Orthodox Church.

Those in whom the desire to learn more about the Orthodox Church is awakened by Vernardakis' *Sacred Catechism*, as presented in this volume, will have this desire gratified to a certain degree by the Supplement which I have added. The texts that constitute it deal with the Architecture of the Orthodox temple known as Byzantine, the Theology of Holy Icons, and the Hymnography of the Church.

Something must be said about certain emendations which I have made in Cobham's translation of Vernardakis' book, in order to bring his translation closer to the Greek text. I list them in alphabetical order:

"adoration of pictures" → veneration of icons
"Christ was made man" → Christ became man
"Councils" → Synods

"Easter" → Pascha

"Evening Prayer" → Vesper Service

"God framed" → God created

"Holy Ghost" → Holy Spirit

"lamps" → sacred lamps

"Mary" → the Holy Virgin Mary

"Morning Prayer" → Orthros

"Mother of God" → Theotokos

"of one substance with the Father" → of one essence with the Father

"original sin" → ancestral sin

"pictures" → icons

"the quick and the dead" → the living and the dead

"Sacramental Supper" → Mystical Supper

"Sacraments" → Mysteria

"Sanctuary" → Holy Bema

"singers" → chanters

"very God of very God" → true God of true God

In presenting the English edition of Vernardakis' *Sacred Catechism*, I have added a detailed Table of Contents, a few notes, a Supplement (pp. 93-126), and a General Index. In the Supplement I explain and illustrate three very important components of the Orthodox Church: its distinctive architecture, iconography, and hymnography. Vernardakis makes brief reference to iconography, but none to architecture and hymnography.

My most grateful thanks are due to the Library of the University of Cincinnati for having provided to me very valuable information with regard to the original Greek edition of Vernardakis' *Sacred Catechism.*

CONSTANTINE CAVARNOS

Belmont, Massachusetts
July, 2003

Demetrios N. Vernardakis

BIOGRAPHICAL NOTE ON DEMETRIOS N. VERNARDAKIS

By

CONSTANTINE CAVARNOS

The deeply religious polymath (historian, theologian, philologist), Demetrios N. Vernardakis, was born in 1833 in the town of Hagia Marina, a suburb of Mytilene, the capital of the historic Aegean Island of Lesvos. He received his elementary education at his native place and his high school education at Athens. After graduating from high school, he attended the School of Philosophy of the University of that famous city. Then he went to Germany and did graduate work at the universities of Munich and Berlin (1856-1861). There he received instruction in the fields of philology, philosophy, history, and literature, and was awarded the degree of Doctor of Philosophy.

When he returned to Greece, he was appointed Assistant Professor of General History and Philology at the University of Athens, and the next year full Professor in the same fields. He taught there from 1861 to 1869, and again during 1882-1883.

Withdrawing from public life in 1883, he went to his native place and lived there until the time of his death in 1907, occupying himself with writing, farming, and counseling people to lead a godly life. For this reason he was called "the hermit of Mytilene." He censured the distancing of society from moral principles, and particularly from the Orthodox Christian Faith.

Vernardakis was a prolific writer. His most noteworthy publications besides the *Catechism* are the following: (1) *General History* (1867). (2) Several works of the ancient Greek dramatist Euripides, with important interpretative scholia and notes (1888-1894). (3) Seven dramas in which he seeks to relate in important ways dramatic poetry to the religious life of the Greek people. (4) *Sacred Catechism.*[1] (5) A monograph on Byzantine Music entitled *Offhand*

[1] Ἱερὰ Κατήχησις, Constantinople, 1870, 1872.

Discourse on Church Music. In this work he extols the value of the traditional, Byzantine music of the Greek Church and strongly criticizes attempts to "modernize" it by introducing elements taken from Western church music, such four-part chant.[1] And (6) *Sacred History.*[2]

Demetrios N. Vernardakis is reckoned among the "Great Educators of Greece," such as Benjamin of Lesvos, Adamantios Korais, and Georgios Gennadios. His biography appears in the *Religious and Ethical Encyclopedia*,[3] and in other Greek Encyclopedias.

[1] Λόγος Αὐτοσχέδιος περὶ τῆς καθ' ἡμᾶς 'Εκκλησιαστικῆς Μουσικῆς, Trieste, 1876, 1884.

[2] Ἱερὰ Ἱστορία, 1872..

[3] Ε. Ν. Μόσχος, "Δημήτριος Βερναρδάκης," Θρησκευτικὴ καὶ 'Ηθικὴ 'Εγκυκλοπαιδεία, Vol. 3, Athens, 1963, pp. 815-816.

CONTENTS

PART ONE

DOGMAS
OR CONCERNING THE CREED

PART TWO

DIVINE WORSHIP
OR CONCERNING
THE DIVINE MYSTERIA

PART THREE

MORALITY
THE TEN COMMANDMENTS

PART FOUR

MORALITY
THE NINE BEATITUDES OF THE GOSPEL

SUPPLEMENT

BY CONSTANTINE CAVARNOS

"The dogmas of the Christian Faith are contained fully in the holy Scripture and in the Tradition of the Church. They are summarized in the Symbol of the Faith, that is, in the Confession of the Faith, which was composed by the First Oecumenical Synod at Nicaea and was completed, from the 8th article to the end, by the Second Oecumenical Synod of Constantinople, and was validated by all subsequent ones."—Introductory statement of Vernardakis, omitted by Cobham, the translator of the *Catechism*.[1]

[1] C. C.

PART ONE

DOGMAS, OR CONCERNING THE CREED

The Articles of the Creed

Question. **How many articles has the Orthodox Creed?**

Answer. **The Creed has twelve articles, as follows:**

I. I believe in one God, Father, Almighty, Creator of heaven and earth, and of all things visible and invisible.

II. And in one Lord Jesus Christ, the only begotten Son of God, begotten of the Father before all the ages, Light of Light, true God of true God, begotten, not made, of one essence with the Father, by Whom all things were made.

III. Who for us men and for our salvation came down from the Heavens and was incarnate of the Holy Spirit and the Virgin Mary, and became man.

IV. And was crucified for us under Pontius Pilate, and suffered and was buried.

V. And rose on the third day according to the Scriptures.

VI. And He ascended into the Heavens, and sitteth at the right hand of the Father.

VII. And He shall come again with glory to judge the living and the dead, of Whose Kingdom there shall be no end.

VIII. And in the Holy Spirit, the Lord, the Giver of life, Who proceedeth from the Father, Who with the Father and the Son together is worshipped and glorified, Who spoke by the Prophets.

IX. In One, Holy, Catholic, and Apostolic Church.

X. I confess one Baptism for the remission of sins.

XI. I expect the resurrection of the dead.

XII. And the life in the age to come.

First Article of the Creed

The Holy Trinity

Ques. **What is the First Thing which we are taught by the very beginning of the Creed?**

Ans. **That there is one God.**

Ques. By what is it proved that God exists?

Ans. It is proved first by our own very self, which neither we ourselves could create, nor can anyone else like us create.

Ques. By what else is it proved?

Ans. It is proved by the whole world, the heaven, the earth, and all things that are, which neither were created of themselves, nor is man able to create them.

Ques. What do you conclude from this?

Ans. I conclude that there exists a Being higher than man and the world, Who created the world and man, and this higher Being is God.

Ques. How many Persons is God?

Ans. God is Three Persons: Father, Son, and Holy Spirit; and these Three Persons are the Holy Trinity. The Three together are one and the same God.

Ques. What else have you to say concerning the Three Persons of the Holy Trinity?

Ans. The First Person of the Holy Trinity, the Father, is uncreated and unbegotten; the Second Person, the Son, is uncreated and begotten of the Father; the Third Person, the Holy Spirit, is uncreated and proceeds from the Father.

Ques. What are the chief attributes of God?

Ans. God is one, immaterial, timeless, eternal, omnipresent, omnipotent, all-good, just, all-wise, and generally He is the beginning and the end of all perfection and virtue.

Ques. What else does the first article of the Creed teach us?

Ans. That God created the heaven and the earth, and all things visible and invisible.

Ques. What are the visible things?

Ans. Visible thing are all we see, such as the earth, the sun, the stars, man, and generally all natural bodies.

Ques. What are the invisible things?

Ans. Invisible things are all we do not see, such as the souls and the angels.

Ques. What are the angels?

Ans. The angels are spirits immaterial who serve God.

Ques. Are there wicked angels?

Ans. There are demons or devils, whom God created good, but since they willed to set themselves against God, God cast them into the outer fire and punishment.

Ques. What is the activity of the demons?

Ans. They endeavor to draw man to evil and sin; not, however, by force, but with falsehood and deceit.

Ques. To what world does man belong, to the visible and material, or to the invisible and immaterial?

Ans. Man has a visible and material body, and by it he belongs to the visible and material world; but he has also an immaterial and immortal soul, and by it he belongs to the immaterial and invisible world.

Ques. What then is man's rank in creation?

Ans. Man is the highest and most perfect of all visible creatures.

Ques. Of what did God make man?

Ans. God made man of earth, and breathed into him an immaterial and immortal soul.

Ques. Into whose likeness did God make man?

Ans. God made man in His own image and likeness.

Ques. What does this mean?

Ans. It means that God bestowed on man all the qualities which God Himself has, but in a far lower measure and degree.

Ques. Why did God make the world and man?

Ans. God made the world and man in His all-goodness, that they might have a part in His good things.

Ques. Where did God set man, and what did He order him to do?

Ans. He set him in Paradise, and gave him power over all beasts and plants. He ordered him only not to eat of the tree of knowledge of good and evil, because he would die and be miserable.

Ques. Did man keep God's command?

Ans. No, the devil in the form of a serpent deceived Eve, Adam's wife, who ate and gave to Adam, and he ate.

Ques. How were Adam and Eve punished for their disobedience?

Ans. They were driven out of Paradise, and from immortal and happy beings they became mortal and miserable.

Ques. In what consisted the former happiness of Adam and Eve?

Ans. In that they were near to God and always willed and did good, never evil.

Ques. In what consisted the later unhappiness of Adam and Eve?

Ans. In that they were removed far from God, Whom they began also to forget, and in that instead of doing good they were inclined more to do evil.

Ques. What do we call the disobedience of Adam and Eve?

Ans. We call it sin.

Ques. Is sin confined to Adam and Eve alone?

Ans. No, it was transmitted to all men, who are descended from them.

Ques. What were the results of sin?

Ans. The results of Adam's and Eve's sin were that man forgot God altogether and was estranged from Him, and that he inclined not to good things which God wills, but to evil things which the devil wills.

Ques. Could not God hinder man from sin by force?

Ans. He could as Almighty, but He would not, because as all-good He had created man with the faculty of free choice and self-control.

Ques. Did not God foresee that man would sin?

Ans. He foresaw it, as He foresees and foreknows all things, both good and bad. Nevertheless, God is not the cause of evil, but the devil, and that man errs who can withstand the devil and avoid evil, and does not do so.

Ques. What means does the devil employ to entice men to sin?

Ans. The fleshy pleasures and enjoyments of man, his evil desires and appetites, and his passions.

Ques. Was it possible for man to be saved and freed by his own effort from the state of sin in which he found himself?

Ans. It was not possible.

Ques. Was he destined then to remain for ever in this state?

Ans. No, because God, as the all-good friend of man, had from the beginning made provision for saving man from sin, when the fitting time should come.

Ques. What is God's Providence?

Ans. We call God's Providence the thought and foresight which God has for the preservation and the good of the whole world.

Ques. What is the Providence of God concerning man?

Ans. That man should be saved from sin without violence done to man's free will.

Ques. How was this possible?

Ans. This was impossible to man, but not to God, Who to this end sent upon earth His only begotten Son to save man from sin.

Ques. How did the Son of God accomplish this salvation?

Ans. By becoming man and dying on the Cross.

Ques. Why did He become man?

Ans. To teach man as man, and thus to do no violence to man's free will.

Ques. What result had the teaching and death of the Son of God?

Ans. The saving of man from sin, which was taken away from man, and pardoned by God.

Ques. Why did not this salvation come sooner?

Ans. Because it was necessary that man should be prepared gradually to accept the teaching of the Son of God.

Ques. What was the Law which prepared man for this?

Ans. The Law which God gave by Moses to the Israelites, and which is contained in the Old Testament.

Second Article of the Creed

Christ

Ques. **What is the Second Article in the Creed?**

Ans. **"And in one Lord Jesus Christ, the only begotten Son of God, begotten of the Father before all the ages, Light of Light, true God of true God, begotten, not made, of one essence with the Father, by Whom all things were made."**

Ques. **What does this second article of the Creed teach us?**

Ans. **It teaches us the attributes of the Second Person of the Holy Trinity, Who is the very Son of God, Who became man and suffered death to save men from sin.**

Ques. What are these attributes of the Second Person?

Ans. That He is the only begotten Son of God, that He was not made by the Father like the creatures, but that He was begotten of Him, Light of Light, and true God of true God, that He is of one essence with the Father, in other words is God, and that through Him the world was made.

Third Article of the Creed

Our Salvation

Ques. **What is the Third Article of the Creed?**

Ans. **"Who for us men and for our salvation came down from the Heavens, and was incarnate of the Holy Spirit and the Virgin Mary, and became man."**

Ques. **What does this article of the Creed teach us?**

Ans. **It teaches us that the Son of God descended from the Heavens, and took a human body from the Virgin Mary by the Holy Spirit, and became man.**

Ques. What else does it teach us?

Ans. That Mary remained a Virgin after the birth of her Child, even as she was before that birth.

Ques. What other name was given to Jesus?

Ans. Christ (Χριστός), which means the Anointed One, because He was anointed, not however by man, as were the kings, priests and prophets of the Israelites, but by the Holy Spirit.

Ques. When the Son of God became man, did he cease to be God?

Ans. No, the Son of God, when He became man remained also God, as He was before; and thus one and the same Person was God-Man, that is at once God and Man.

Ques. As Jesus Christ has two natures, has He also two wills?

Ans. Yes, one as God and one as man. The human will is however subjected to the Divine.

Ques. The life and doings of Jesus Christ, were they divine and human?

Ans. Some were divine and others human, He lived as other men, but worked miracles as God.

Ques. Give some instances.

Ans. For instance, when He wept for Lazarus, He wept as man; but when He raised Lazarus from the grave He raised him as God.

Ques. Give another instance.

Ans. When He slept in Peter's ship, He slept as man; but when He walked on the sea, He walked as God.

Ques. Another.

Ans. When He was persecuted by His enemies and was condemned to death and died and was buried, He suffered as man; but when after three days He rose from the dead He rose as God.

Fourth Article of the Creed

The Crucifixion

Ques. **What is the Fourth Article of the Creed?**

Ans. **"He was crucified for us under Pontius Pilate, and suffered, and was buried."**

Ques. **What does this article teach us?**

Ans. **That Jesus Christ was persecuted by the chief priests and scribes in the days of the Governor of Judaea, Pontius Pilate, and that He was condemned and crucified, and died and was buried.**

Fifth Article of the Creed

The Resurrection

Ques. **What is the Fifth Article of the Creed?**

Ans. **"And He rose on the third day according to the Scriptures."**

Ques. **What does this article teach us?**

Ans. **That Jesus Christ when He died on the Cross as man, descended as God into Hades, and preached salvation to the souls there, and after three days He rose as God from the grave.**

Sixth Article of the Creed

The Ascension

Ques. **What is the Sixth Article of the Creed?**

Ans. **"And He ascended into the Heavens and sitteth on the right hand of the Father."**

Ques. **What does this article teach us?**

Ans. **That Jesus Christ was taken up into Heaven forty days after His resurrection.**

Ques. What did Jesus Christ do on earth during forty days?

Ans. He appeared to His disciples, whom He commanded to go out into the world and to teach His Gospel.

Ques. What else did He command them?

Ans. To baptise all who believed in the name of the Father, and of the Son, and of the Holy Spirit. He gave them also authority to forgive sins.

Ques. How was Jesus Christ taken up into Heaven, as God, or as man with His human body?

Ans. With His human body, because as God He existed always, in Heaven and everywhere.

Seventh Article of the Creed

The Second Coming of Christ

Ques. **What is the Seventh Article of the Creed?**

Ans. **"And shall come again with glory to judge the living and the dead, of Whose Kingdom there shall be no end."**

Ques. **What does this article teach us?**

Ans. **It teaches us that our Savior Jesus Christ shall appear once again to judge all the world, both the living and the dead.**

Ques. When and how will this Second Coming of Christ be?

Ans. When the consummation comes, that is, the end of the world, then the souls of the dead will be united to their bodies, and together with all that are alive, will be caught up suddenly, and will appear before Christ, that He may judge them.

Ques. Will this Second Coming of Christ be like the First?

Ans. No, because at His First Coming He appeared to men as a lowly man, while at His Second He will come with all His Glory and Might and Majesty, as God.

Ques. After what manner will be the Judgment of men and their Retribution?

Ans. On the right hand of the throne where Christ shall sit will be set the just and virtuous, and on the left hand sinners and wicked men. And after telling the first all the good things they did He shall send them to everlasting joy and life and blessedness; but the others, after telling them all the bad things they did, He shall send into the outer fire, where they will be punished.

Eighth Article of the Creed

The Holy Spirit

Ques. **What is the Eighth Article of the Creed?**

Ans. **"And in the Holy Spirit, the Lord, the Giver of life, Who proceedeth from the Father, Who with the Father and the Son together is worshipped and glorified, Who spoke by the Prophets."**

Ques. **What does this article of the Creed teach us?**

Ans. **It teaches us the attributes of the Third Person of the Holy Trinity, that is the Holy Spirit, mentioned also at the beginning of the Creed.**

Ques. Why is it said that the Holy Spirit is the Giver of life, and that He spoke by the Prophets?

Ans. Because the Holy Spirit gives Divine grace and life to man, and because He spoke by the mouth of the Prophets all that they said and wrote.

Ques. What are the effects of the Divine grace and life which the Holy Spirit gives to man?

Ans. The enlightenment of the mind and the sanctification of the heart of man.

Ques. What spiritual gifts does man acquire with the enlightenment of his mind?

Ans. He sees and understands things which without the Divine grace it would be impossible for him to see and understand.

Ques. What spiritual gift does man acquire with the sanctification of his heart?

Ans. He draws near to God and is thus strengthened to overcome the devil and to flee from sin, and to desire and do what is good.

Ques. Can all men acquire the grace of the Holy Spirit?

Ans. All have the power, but not all have the will so to do.

Ques. Why?

Ans. Because the Holy Spirit gives the Divine grace to those who are worthy; and in order that a man may become worthy he must have the fear of God and great faith and devotion towards Him, to which very few attain.

Ques. Were only the Prophets found worthy of the grace of the Holy Spirit?

Ans. No. Many other holy and saintly men of the Old Dispensation.

Ques. What others?

Ans. First and chiefest of all, the Disciples and Apostles of Jesus Christ, on whose heads the Holy Spirit descended in the shape of flames of fire on the fiftieth day [Penetecost] after the Resurrection of Christ.

Ques. What others in a lesser degree?

Ans. The holy Fathers of the Church who assembled in the Oecumenical Synods.

The Seven Oecumenical Synods

Ques. What is an Oecumenical Synod?

Ans. An Oecumenical Synod is a meeting of the holy Fathers and Teachers of the Church from all parts of the world to discuss and decide questions of the Christian faith.

Ques. How many such Oecumenical Synods have there been?

Ans. Seven. The first of these compiled the Creed.

Holy Tradition

Ques. All things that holy men, enlightened and guided by the Holy Spirit, said, are they written, or did some remain unwritten?

Ans. Some remained unwritten, which have been preserved in the Church by Tradition from the time of the Apostles until today.

Ques. Give some examples.

Ans. That we should turn to the East in prayer; that we should make the sign of the cross; that priests should wear a peculiar dress; that we should light sacred lamps in the Church; and many others.

NINTH ARTICLE OF THE CREED

The Church

Ques. **What is the Ninth Article of the Creed?**

Ans. **"In one Holy, Catholic, and Apostolic Church."**

Ques. **What does this article of the Creed teach us?**

Ans. **It teaches us the attributes of the Church of Christ.**

Ques. What are these attributes?

Ans. That the Church of Christ is one, and not many; that it is holy, because it was sanctified by Christ; that it is Apostolic, because it is governed and administered according to the teaching and Tradition of the Apostles; that it is Catholic (Universal), because it is world-wide and makes no distinction of places and races.

Ques. What is it that we call the Church?

Ans. By the Church we mean the whole body of Christians, that is, the whole body of men, women, and children who believe in Jesus Christ, have been baptized in the name of the Holy Trinity, and believe what Holy Scripture, Tradition, and the Seven Oecumenical Synods teach.

Ques. Who is the Head, and who are the Members of the Church?

Ans. The Head of the Church is Christ, and all Orthodox Christians are its Members.

Ques. Who governs and administers the Church?

Ans. The Bishops and their representatives, Presbyters or Priests who receive the gift of Orders from the Bishops, who derived it in succession from the Apostles.

Ques. What is the work of the Bishops and Priests?

Ans. First, to preach the Word of God; secondly, to administer the Divine Mysteria; and thirdly, to govern the Church.

Ques. When was the Church of Christ first established?

Ans. It was established first of all in the time of Christ and His Apostles at Jerusalem, and thence gradually through the preaching of the Apostles and their successors it has been spread abroad in all the world.

Ques. Did the Church suffer persecutions and wars?

Ans. The Church suffered many fearful and murderous persecutions, in which Christians who would not deny Christ were killed, after they had suffered many savage and terrible torments.

Ques. Who are these brave Christians who preferred to be tortured and put to death rather than deny Christ?

Ans. They are the holy Martyrs of Christ.

Ques. What other kind of persecutions has the Church suffered?

Ans. It has suffered from within the persecutions by heretics, which were even worse than the persecutions by idolaters from without.

Ques. What did these heretics seek to do with their heresies?

Ans. They sought to cast out from the Church the doctrines which it had received from Christ and from the Apostles, and to bring in their own false and blasphemous doctrines.

Ques. Was it only of old time that there were such heresies and heretics, or do they exist even now?

Ans. They exist, unhappily, even now, in very great numbers.

Ques. What are the greatest of these heresies?

Ans. The first is the heresy of the Latins, Westerns, or Papists, who have been separated from the true Church of Christ, and are subject to the Pope of Rome.

Ques. What other?

Ans. Next are the Protestants, who have been separated from the Pope, and are no longer subject to him. They are subdivided into Lutherans, Calvinists, and numberless other heresies.

Ques. Which is the true Church of Christ?

Ans. The only true Church is the Eastern Orthodox Church.

Ques. Why is this Church commonly called "Eastern?"

Ans. Because most of the Christians of this Church live in the East.

Ques. Why is it called Orthodox?

Ans. Because it judges rightly (*orthós*), that is, it professes and teaches the true dogmas of the Christian Faith, as it received them from Christ, and from the Apostles, and as the Seven Oecumenical Synods explained them.

Ques. Who are the spiritual chiefs of the Orthodox Church?

Ans. The Patriarch of Constantinople, and the Patriarchs of Jerusalem, Antioch, and Alexandria.[1]

[1] Vernardakis lists only the ancient Patriarchates. Besides these there is the Patriarchate of Russia, that of Serbia, that of Rumania, that of Bulgaria, and that of Georgia, which are later. (C.C.)

Tenth Article of the Creed

Holy Baptism

Ques. **What is the Tenth Article of the Creed?**

Ans. **"I acknowledge one Baptism for the remission of sins."**

Ques. **What does this tenth article teach us?**

Ans. **That the Christian's faith is not sufficient if he does not also receive Baptism, which is one of the Seven Divine Mysteria, touching which the Second Part of this Catechism will treat.**

Eleventh Article of the Creed

The Resurrection of the Dead

Ques. **What is the Eleventh Article of the Creed?**

Ans. **"I expect the resurrection of the dead."**

Ques. **What does this article teach us?**

Ans. **That the dead shall live again at the Second Coming of Christ, as we have learned.**

Twelfth Article of the Creed

The Future Life

Ques. **What is the Twelfth Article of the Creed?**

Ans. **"And a life in the age to come. *Amen*."**

Ques. **What does this twelfth article teach us?**

Ans. **That after the Second Coming of Christ there shall follow a life eternal, unending, bringing joy and happiness to the just and virtuous, but suffering to sinners.**

PART TWO

DIVINE WORSHIP, OR CONCERNING THE DIVINE MYSTERIA

Ques. **What have we been taught so far in Part One of the Catechism?**

Ans. **We have been taught the Dogmas of the Christian Faith, that is, what a Christian must believe in order to find his salvation.**

Ques. What is the Christian's salvation?

Ans. To be saved from sin, that he may enjoy hereafter eternal life and bliss.

Ques. **What are we to be taught in Part Two of the Catechism?**

Ans. **We shall be taught how a Christian must worship God.**

Worship

Ques. **What do you mean by Divine Worship?**

Ans. **The manifesting by outward signs our faith in God.**

Ques. By Divine Worship do we only make outward show of our faith, or do we acquire also Divine Grace?

Ans. Yes, indeed, we acquire also Divine Grace through the Holy Spirit.

Ques. What are the most important forms of worship by which we acquire Divine Grace?

Ans. The Divine Mysteria.

Ques. How many are the Divine Mysteria, and which are they?

Ans. Seven: (i) Holy Baptism, (ii) Holy Chrism, (iii) Divine Communion or Eucharist, (iv) Confession, (v) Holy Orders, (vi) Holy Matrimony, and (vii) Evchelaion.

Ques. By whom and where are the Holy Mysteria celebrated?

Ans. By the priests, in the temple of God, the church.

Ques. What do you mean by a sacred rite?

Ans. All the sacred acts, such as the prayers and supplications of the priest and of the faithful, by which the administration of the Holy Mysteria is accompanied, come under the term "sacred rite."

Ques. How is prayer offered in the church, aloud or in thought?

Ans. Aloud, by the priests sometimes, by the chanters always; the rest of the faithful follow the prayers of the priests and the thanksgivings of the chanters with silent prayer.

The Divine Liturgy

Ques. **What is the chief rite of the Church?**

Ans. **The Divine Liturgy, in which is celebrated the Mysterion of the Divine Eucharist.**

Ques. Speaking generally, what is a Service?

Ans. A Service is the whole body of prayers and thanksgivings which the priests and chanters read and chant before God in the church.

Ques. The chief services (*akolouthiai*) of the Church, which Christians ought especially to attend, how many are they?

Ans. Three: **Vespers**, towards the evening, **Orthros**, about the dawn, and the **Divine Liturgy**, after Orthros.

Ques. When is the Divine Liturgy celebrated?

Ans. Every day, with the exception of certain fixed days, but indispensably every Sunday, the day which is kept as a feast in memory and honor Christ's resurrection, and on every feast of Christ, of the Theotokos, and of the other Saints.

The Divine Mysteria

(1) Holy Baptism

Ques. **What is the first Mysterion, and how is it celebrated?**

Ans. **The first Mysterion is Baptism, which was ordained by Christ Himself. In this Mysterion the Christian is immersed in water three times, in the Name of the Father, and of the Son, and of the Holy Spirit.**

Ques. What is the Divine Grace which the Christian acquires with Holy Baptism?

Ans. With Holy Baptism, which he receives only once in his life, the Christian is cleansed from ancestral sin and from all sins into which he has fallen before he was baptised, and he becomes at the same time a member of the Church of Christ.

Ques. What is required before a person be baptised?

Ans. It is required that he should renounce the devil and his works, that is, sin, and confess that he has full faith in Jesus Christ.

Ques. How does the person about to be baptized make this confession of faith?

Ans. He recites the Creed, in which is contained the Christian Faith.

Ques. How, then, are infants baptized, when by reason of their age they cannot have faith in Christ?

Ans. They are baptised because the *sponsor* (*anádochos*) recites, as the representative of the infants, the Creed, and accepts before God and men the promise and obligation to teach and catechise, if necessary, the children who are baptized, when they come to an age to understand.

(2) Holy Chrism

Ques. **What is the second Holy Mysterion?**

Ans. **Holy Chrism, with which are anointed the chief members of the body of the person who has been baptised.**

Ques. What is the meaning and aim of Holy Chrism?

Ans. With the Holy Chrism the person baptized receives the gifts of the Holy Spirit, by which he advances in every good work.

(3) Divine Eucharist

***Ques*. What is the third Holy Mysterion?**

***Ans*. The third Holy Mysterion is the Divine Eucharist, which is also called Holy Communion. Our Lord Jesus Christ instituted this Mysterion when He ate for the last time before the Passover with His disciples at the Mystical Supper.**

Ques. What did Christ do, and what did He say at the Mystical Supper?

Ans. He took bread, and when He had broken it, He divided it among His disciples and said: "Take, eat, this is My Body." Then He took the cup with wine and gave it to His disciples, saying: "Drink of this all of you, this is My Blood. Do this always in remembrance of Me."

Ques. By whom, when, and where is the Mysterion of the Eucharist celebrated?

Ans. By the priest in the Divine Liturgy on the Holy Table which is in the midst of the Holy Bema of the church.

Ques. How is this Holy Mysterion celebrated, and how do Christians communicate in it?

Ans. The priest takes bread, and wine with water, which through the prayers of the priest, and the devotions and supplications of the Church, are changed by the Holy Spirit, and the bread becomes the Body of Christ, and the wine His Blood. Thus the Christian partakes of the very Body and Blood of Christ, even though the Holy Communion has the taste not of flesh and blood, but of bread and wine.

Ques. What is the aim of this Holy Mysterion?

Ans. The Christian partaking of the sacred Body and Blood of our Savior Christ is made one with Him, and thus acquires the strongest weapon against the devil and sin, and is sanctified and strengthened to do works good and pleasing to God.

Ques. How often should a Christian partake of the Holy Communion?

Ans. As often as possible, if he is able; but it is hard to be always ready for and worthy of the Holy Communion. The Christian should receive Holy Communion at least four times a year, after first fasting during the four fasts: before Christmas, Pascha, the Holy Apostles, and the Dormition of the Theotokos.

Ques. What is the preparation which is required of the Christian before he receives Holy Communion?

Ans. He ought to examine himself, to see what sins he has committed; to be deeply sorry for them; to repent sincerely; and to determine steadfastly and inexorably that he will sin no more.

Ques. Then what should he do?

Ans. Go to his Spiritual Father, to whom he should confess all his sins, without hiding through fear or shame the least of them; assure him that he has repented; and if the sins are venial, the Spiritual Father forgives them and gives the person who confesses them leave to receive Holy Communion. If, however, they are serious, he repels him until he has fulfilled the ecclesiastical penances which he imposes on the confessant.

Ques. Is the Holy Mysterion of the Eucharist necessary to salvation?

Ans. The Christian cannot be saved unless he receives Holy Communion. However, he must be prepared, as we have said, because as much benefit as Holy Communion brings to him who receives it worthily, so much injury it brings to him who receives it unworthily.

(4) Repentance and Confession

Ques. **What is the fourth Holy Mysterion, and what is its meaning?**

Ans. **The fourth Holy Mysterion is Repentance and Confession. In this Mysterion he who confesses his sins and repents of them from the depth of his soul and heart, invokes the mercy of God, and through the priest receives from God the forgiveness of his sins.**

Ques. From whom has the priest authority to forgive sins?

Ans. The priest receives this authority from the Bishop, who has it in succession from the Apostles. Our Lord Jesus Christ Himself gave this authority to the Apostles.

(5) Holy Orders

Ques. **What is the fifth Holy Mysterion, and what is its meaning?**

Ans. **The fifth Holy Mysterion is Holy Orders. In this Holy Mysterion the Bishop, laying his hands on the candidate, imparts to him from the Holy Spirit the gift of Holy Orders.**

Ques. What is the ministry of the priesthood?

Ans. The preaching of the word of God, the governance of the Church, and, above all, the celebration of the Holy Mysteria.

Ques. From whom have the Bishops received power and authority to confer the gift of Holy Orders?

Ans. By succession from the Apostles.

Ques. Who have the full dignity of Holy Orders and who do not?

Ans. Priests have the full dignity of Holy Orders, and Bishops who confer it on priests, who are subordinate to them. But Deacons have not the grace of Holy Orders in full. They help the Bishop and the priest in the celebration of the Holy Mysteria, but deacons have not power to celebrate a Holy Mysterion.

(6) Holy Matrimony

Ques. **What is the sixth Holy Mysterion, and what is done in it?**

Ans. **The sixth Holy Mysterion is Matrimony. In this Holy Mysterion, when the persons betrothed confess their mutual love and determination to be joined together in an honorable marriage, the priest blesses the marriage, and invokes the Divine Grace upon them.**

Ques. What are the duties of husband and wife?

Ans. The husband should love his wife as his very self, and the wife should love her husband and be subject to him as her head, and both should preserve their marriage honorable, and the bed undefiled, and bring up their children in the fear and love of God.

(7) Holy Evchelaion

Ques. **What is the seventh Holy Mysterion, and what is its effect?**

Ans. **The seventh Holy Mysterion is the Evchelaion ("Prayer-oil"), in which the sick person is anointed with oil, and the priest invokes the Divine Grace, which heals the infirmities of soul and body.**

PART THREE

MORALITY
THE TEN COMMANDMENTS

Introductory Remarks

Ques. **What have we been taught so far in the First and Second Parts of the Catechism?**

Ans. **In Part One we have been taught what we ought to believe; in Part Two, how we ought to worship God.**

Ques. **What remains then for us to be taught in Part Three of the Catechism?**

Ans. **There remains for us to be taught what we must do to obey the will of God.**

Ques. Where has God made known His will?

Ans. In the Divine Law, which is contained briefly in the *Decalogue*, or the *Ten Commandments*[1]

[1] Exodus 20:1-17, Deuteronomy 5:6-21. (C. C.)

which God gave to Moses upon Mount Sinai, and in the *Nine Beatitudes* of the Gospel.

Ques. What does God's Law teach us?

Ans. To do good works and avoid evil works, that is, sin.

Ques. Is it only God's Law which teaches us to do good and avoid evil?

Ans. No, but also *conscience*, which is inborn in the heart of every man.

Ques. What is conscience?

Ans. Conscience is the inmost feeling of our heart which makes us grieve when we do evil and rejoice when we do good.

Ques. Does conscience suffice to show us how to avoid evil and to do good?

Ans. No; because it is imperfect, and is corrupted by sin.

Ques. Are *good works* necessary to the Christian's salvation?

Ans. Certainly; because that a Christian be saved it is not enough that he have faith, it is not enough that he be partaker of the Holy and Immaculate Mysteria, but he must also live agreeably with God's commands.

Ques. Tell me in two words *what God's Law teaches us.*

Ans. First, to *love God*, and secondly to *love our neighbor as ourselves.*

The Ten Commandments

I. I am the Lord thy God. Thou shalt have no other gods but Me.

II. Thou shalt not make a graven image, nor the likeness of anything that is in the heaven above, or in the earth beneath, or in the waters under the earth. Thou shalt not bow down to them, nor worship them.

III. Thou shalt not take the name of the Lord thy God in vain.

IV. Remember that thou keep holy the Sabbath day. Six days shalt thou labor and do all thy work, but the seventh day is a Sabbath unto the Lord thy God.

V. Honor thy father and thy mother, that thou mayest prosper and live long upon the earth.

VI. Do not kill.

VII. Do not commit adultery.

VIII. Do not steal.

IX. Do not bear false witness against thy neighbor.

X. Do not covet thy neighbor's wife. Do not covet thy neighbor's house, nor his field, nor his servant, nor his maid, nor his ox, nor his beast of burden, nor anything that is thy neighbor's.

The First Commandment

***Ques.* What is the First Commandment of the Decalogue?**

Ans. "I am the Lord thy God. Thou shalt have no other gods but Me."

***Ques.* What does this Commandment teach us?**

***Ans.* It teaches us that we must have no other god besides the one and only true God, that very God Who of old brought the Israelites out of Egypt, and freed them from the enslaving yoke of the Egyptians.**

Ques. What duty flows from this Commandment?

Ans. Our duty to acknowledge the existence of this true God and His attributes, as we were taught them in the Creed.

Ques. What will one feel who studies well these attributes of God?

Ans. Fear and love towards God. Fear, because God is almighty and a Judge of right, Who punishes every sin. Love, because God is kind and all-good, Who not only created man and gave him so many bodily and spiritual blessings, but cares always for him as a Father.

Ques. What else will he feel?

Ans. He will feel that God is the only being to whom he must devote himself wholly, with the body and the soul, and to Him he must dedicate all his trust, his faith, and his hope.

Ques. What then must we do when we feel all this?

Ans. We must turn to God, as children to our Father, open our hearts to Him, and tell Him what we feel.

Ques. What will the fear and love which we have for our Heavenly Father make us say to Him?

Ans. First, we shall glorify Him and thank Him for all the good He has done to us.

Ques. And next?

Ans. We shall beseech Him to keep us as His children.

Ques. And thirdly?

Ans. To help us with His Divine Grace to obey His Holy Will.

Ques. Fourthly?

Ans. To show Himself forgiving and merciful to our faults, promising that we too will display the same forgivingness and mercy to those who err and trespass against us.

Ques. Sixthly?

Ans. To deliver us from the snares of the devil and from sin.

Ques. And lastly?

Ans. To confess His everlasting kingdom and power and glory.

Ques. Is there any prayer which recites all these things which you have just said?

Ans. There is, and it is called *The Lord's Prayer*.

Ques. Why is it called The Lord's Prayer?

Ans. Because our Lord Jesus Christ taught us to offer to our Heavenly Father this very prayer. The prayer is as follows:

"Our Father Who art in the Heavens, hallowed be Thy name, Thy Kingdom come. Thy will be done, as in Heaven so on earth. Give us this day our daily bread, and forgive us our debts as we also forgive our debtors. And lead us not into temptation, but deliver us from the evil one."

Ques. Must we say only this one prayer to God?

Ans. Not this prayer only, but we must pray to God always. And when we have glorified Him and thanked Him we must ask Him for what we need.

Ques. What ought we to ask in prayer from God?

Ans. Not evil things, for this would be insult and blasphemy to God, but things good and agreeable to His Law.

Ques. When and where ought we to pray?

Ans. Always and everywhere. But it is our special duty to pray in the morning when we rise from our beds, when we sit down to table to eat and when we rise from it, and before we lie down to sleep.

Ques. Ought we to pray only at home and in private?

Ans. No, we ought to go often to church, in order to praise God there together with our other Christian brethren.

Ques. When is it our special duty to go to church?

Ans. Always when there is a service, but particularly on Sunday to the Divine Liturgy.

Ques. Who sin against God's First Commandment?

Ans. 1. **Atheists,** who deny God.

2. **Idolaters**, who believe in many and false gods.

3. **Heretics**.

4. **All who deny Divine Providence.**

5. **Magicians** and suchlike people who hope or promise to do miracles through the power of the devil.

6. **Superstitious persons,** who expect God's grace and help from material things and diverse chance signs.

Ques. Who else sin against the First Commandment?

Ans. **All who set all their hopes on anyone but God**. Such as these are all who deify men or material objects.

Ques. Who are these?

Ans. All who devote themselves body and soul to one man or to many men, because they have authority and power, or wealth, or some other advantage.

Ques. Are there others such?

Ans. All who devote themselves body and soul to themselves, and set all their faith and hope on their authority and power, or on their natural gifts, or on their wealth.

Ques. Do we sin against this Commandment when we invoke the Theotokos, or the other Saints?

Ans. We do not sin, because we do not view these holy persons as God, we only invoke them to intercede for us with Him.

The Second Commandment

Ques. **What is the Second Commandment?**

Ans. **"Thou shalt not make a graven image, nor the likeness of anything that is in the heaven above, or in the earth below, or in the waters under the earth. Thou shall not bow down to them, nor worship them."**

Ques. **What does the Second Commandment forbid?**

Ans. It forbids idolatry.

Ques. What is idolatry?

Ans. It is to deify and worship idols, or statues or other likenesses of false gods.

Ques. Who sin against this Commandment?

Ans. Those who worship idols and those who offer worship to themselves. Such are the sensual, the covetous, the proud, and generally all who worship their fleshy desires and pleasures, or passions.

Ques. Does veneration of holy icons transgress this Commandment?

Ans. No, because we do not offer *worship* to the icons of Christ, the Theotokos, and the other Saints, but *honor and reverence*, and this, too, is offered to the *person* of Christ Himself, the Theotokos, and the other Saints of God.

The Third Commandment

Ques. **What is the Third Commandment?**

Ans. **"Thou shalt not take the name of the Lord thy God in vain."**

Ques. **What does this Commandment teach us?**

Ans. **That we should use the name of God with all reverence and awe.**

Ques. Who sin against this Commandment?

Ans. Blasphemers; and these are not only persons who utter insults to God or to things divine, but also all who for any reason whatever murmur or complain against God, as well as those who curse or blaspheme men.

Ques. What others?

Ans. Those who take an oath about trifling, unimportant matters, those who swear falsely, and those who fail in and leave undone what they have promised under oath.

Ques. What others?

Ans. Those who use the name of God mechanically or hypocritically in their prayers, and those who ask of God things which are unseemly or even wicked, as well as those who use God's name lyingly and deceitfully.

The Fourth Commandment

Ques. **What is the Fourth Commandment?**

Ans. **"Remember that thou keep holy the Sabbath day. Six days shalt thou labor and do all thy work, but the seventh day is a Sabbath unto the Lord thy God."**

Ques. **What does this Commandment teach us?**

Ans. **It teaches us that a man ought to work all the week, but on the seventh day to stop all work and consecrate it to God.**

Ques. Which is the Seventh Day?

Ans. For the Jews it was Saturday, because on that day God rested from the creation of the world; but for Christians it is Sunday, because on that day took place Christ's resurrection.

Ques. What are the duties which this commandment teaches us?

Ans. It teaches us that we are bound not only not to work on Sunday, and on the other feasts which the Church has honored as days of rest, but also to devote the whole day to God.

Ques. What then should we do on those days?

Ans. We should go to church, to hear and to meditate on the Word of God, and, when we can, we should do works dear and pleasing to God.

Ques. What are these works which are dear and pleasing to God?

Ans. They are alms, gifts to churches, hospitals, schools, and many other such things.

Ques. Who sin against this Commandment?

Ans. All who without inevitable necessity work on Sunday, or fail to go to church, and all who read books which are not books of piety and spiritually useful, but soul-destroying and deadly.

Ques. What others?

Ans. All who can do alms or contribute to works of common usefulness, and do not do so; all who frequent dances or unseemly spectacles, and all who give themselves up to drunkenness and dissoluteness.

The Fifth Commandment

Ques. **What is the Fifth Commandment?**

Ans. **"Honor thy father and thy mother, that thou mayest prosper and live long upon the earth."**

Ques. **What duties does the Fifth Commandment teach us?**

Ans. **That we should reverence, honor, obey, and love our parents, that we should help them when they are poor, and cherish them in old age, passing over their senile weaknesses. All these things we should do with pleasure and good will, not crossly or grudgingly.**

Ques. To whom besides do we owe the same honor, obedience, and help?

Ans. To our country and our king, to the teachers and pastors of the Church, to our professors and masters, to the ruler and chief men of the state, to elders, to our benefactors, and to our patrons and guardians.

Ques. Is it only children who have duties to their parents, or have parents also duties to their children?

Ans. Parents, too, should help and defend their children in every way, nourish them while they are of tender age, and bring them up in the nurture and admonition of the Lord.

Ques. What are the duties of the king, of those in authority, and spiritual pastors?

Ans. The king and those in authority must take thought for the safety and just treatment of the citizens, as do the spiritual pastors for the admonition and salvation of the souls of their flocks.

The Sixth Commandment

Ques. **What is the Sixth Commandment?**

Ans. **"Thou shalt not kill."**

Ques. **What does this Commandment teach us?**

Ans. **That we ought not to take away the life of our neighbor, and that as love towards our neighbor is our first duty, so the taking away of our neighbor's life is the first of sins and crimes.**

Ques. Who sin against this Commandment?

Ans. Not only those who take their neighbor's life with arms or poison, or in any other way, but those also who, having the power, do not use it to prevent murder.

Ques. What others?

Ans. All who are able to save from death the poor, the hungry and naked and do not do it.

Ques. What others?

Ans. All who cherish in themselves, or excite in others, the causes of murder, to wit, envy, passion and hatred.

Ques. Who are those?

Ans. All who sow scandals and divisions among men, and excite their passions and hate by various means.

Ques. Who else sin against the Sixth Commandment?

Ans. Suicides, persons who kill themselves, all who take bribes, or for any other reason condemn the innocent and acquit the guilty, as well as those who in a court of justice deny or conceal the truth.

The Seventh Commandment

Ques. **What is the Seventh Commandment?**

Ans. **"Do not commit adultery."**

Ques. **What does this Commandment teach us?**

Ans. **That we should not impair our neighbor's honor by causing in any way whatever an interruption of the mutual wedded confidence and love of a man and his wife.**

Ques. Who sin against this commandment?

Ans. All who allow themselves in any fleshly intercourse whatever besides that of lawful marriage.

Ques. What others?

Ans. All who admit, either in themselves or others, words, deeds and sights which serve as a cause or occasion of any shameful act.

Ques. What are these?

Ans. Filthy talk, reading filthy or wanton books, going to filthy or wanton shows, the wanton adornments and dresses of fashion, unseemly movements of the body, drunkenness, gluttony, and evil company.

Eighth Commandment

Ques. **What is the Eighth Commandment?**

Ans. **"Do not steal."**

Ques. **What does this Commandment teach us?**

Ans. **That we must not take from our neighbor's property either much or little, nor for any purpose whatever, either good or evil.**

Ques. Who sin against this Commandment?

Ans. Not only robbers and thieves, but all who by any kind of fraud or lying or injustice seize or alienate the property of another.

Ques. Who else?

Ans. Usurers, coiners, men who use false weights or measures, all who adulterate or over-value their wares, especially grains in time of dearth. All who steal what does not belong to them on occasion of fire or other disturbance, and all who withhold or keep down the wages of their laborers or servants.

Ques. What others?

Ans. Judges who for bribes or other reasons condemn the poor and unprotected, and justify the rich and powerful, and generally rulers and public servants who misuse their authority and position for private ends.

The Ninth Commandment

Ques. **What is the Ninth Commandment?**

Ans. **"Do not bear false witness against thy neighbor."**

Ques. **What does this Commandment teach us?**

Ans. **Never to tell a lie to our neighbor's harm. But even though we may not have this intention, a lie is always unpardonable; we must everywhere and always tell the truth.**

Ques. Who sin against this Commandment?

Ans. All who are summoned to a Court as witnesses and do not tell the truth but a lie, and thus are the cause that the guilty man is acquitted and the innocent is put to death, or injured in his property, his honor, or reputation.

Ques. Who else?

Ans. All who falsely charge any one before a court, as well as judges who condemn the innocent and acquit the guilty.

Ques. Who else?

Ans. Hypocrites, evil speakers, slanderers, tattlers, and all who traduce the honor and reputation of another in any indirect or crooked way.

Ques. Who else?

Ans. All who envy their neighbor, because all the sins of which we have just spoken of are generally bred of envy, which moves a man to displeasure over the material or spiritual good things which his neighbor enjoys.

The Tenth Commandment

Ques. **What is the Tenth Commandment?**

Ans. **Do not covet thy neighbor's wife. Do not covet thy neighbor's house, nor his field, nor his servant, nor his maid, nor his ox, nor his beast of burden, nor his donkey, nor anything that is thy neighbor's."**

Ques. **What does this Commandment teach us?**

Ans. **That we must not covet any of our neighbor's goods, because the desire to seize a thing which is not ours makes a man become a murderer, an adulterer, a thief, and a liar.**

The General Purpose of The Ten Commandments

The purpose of these Ten Commandments is, as was said before, that a man should acquire love towards God and love towards his neighbor. The end of love towards God is to make a man pious and obedient to God's law. And the end of love towards one's neighbor is that a man should not hurt his neighbor, either in his life, or his honor, or his property. For whoso loves his neighbor as himself does not wish to do to his neighbor that which he would not have his neighbor do to him.

Christ's Teaching

These Ten Commandments are not sufficient for the Christian who wishes to be perfect. They are not sufficient, because the teaching of Jesus Christ is still higher than the teaching of the Old Testament, and requires that the Christian shall love his neighbor better than his own self, and shall prefer even to suffer, rather than do wrong to him.

The teaching of Christ is concisely contained in the Nine Beatitudes.

Christ Blessing

Icon by the hand of Photios Kontoglou. 1952.

PART FOUR

MORALITY
THE NINE BEATITUDES

List of the Beatitudes[1]

I. **"Blessed are the poor in spirit: for theirs is the Kingdom of Heaven."**

II. **"Blessed are they that mourn: for they shall be comforted."**

III. **"Blessed are the meek: for they shall inherit the earth."**

IV. **"Blessed are they that hunger and thirst after righteousness: for they shall be filled."**

V. **"Blessed are the merciful: for they shall obtain mercy."**

VI. **"Blessed are the pure in heart: for they shall see God."**

VII. **"Blessed are the peacemakers: for they shall be called sons of God."**

[1] *The Gospel According to St. Matthew,* 5:3-12. (C.C.)

VIII. **"Blessed are they that are persecuted for righteousness' sake: for theirs is the Kingdom of Heaven."**

IX. **"Blessed are ye, when men shall revile you, and persecute you, and shall say all manner of evil against you falsely, for My sake. Rejoice, and be exceeding glad: for great is your reward in Heaven."**

The First Beatitude

"Blessed are the poor in spirit: for theirs is the Kingdom of Heaven."

Ques. What is the meaning of the First Beatitude?

Ans. Since pride is the first of sins, which cast down the devil, and which is for man also the cause of the greatest evils, for this reason our Savior says that blessed and happy are the poor in spirit, that is the humble-minded, for theirs is the Kingdom of Heaven.

Ques. What is the Kingdom of Heaven?

Ans. The eternal life and blessedness, which the devil lost, and which all the proud will lose, and the humble-minded will gain.

The Second Beatitude

"Blessed are they that mourn: for they shall be comforted."

Ques. What is the meaning of the Second Beatitude?

Ans. Jesus Christ calls blessed all who mourn and are sorry for their sins, for they shall be comforted. For God turns away only from the unrepentant, not from those who repent sincerely.

The Third Beatitude

"Blessed are the meek: for they shall inherit the earth."

Ques. What is the meaning of the Third Beatitude?

Ans. Since the world commonly believed that the earth is governed by fierce passions, by war and blood shedding, the Savior calls blessed those who have no fierce passions, but are gentle and temperate, and says that they shall inherit the earth. And in very deed those who are called Christ's Apostles, without the sword, and only by the Gospel, inherited the world.

The Fourth Beatitude

"Blessed are they that hunger and thirst after righteousness: for they shall be filled."

Ques. What is the meaning of the Fourth Beatitude?

Ans. Since the world usually thinks that those who are wronged are unhappy, Jesus Christ on the contrary tells us that not they who do wrong are happy, but they who are wronged, for they shall enjoy in Heaven a hundredfold what they lost on earth through injustice and wrong.

The Fifth Beatitude

"Blessed are the merciful: for they shall obtain mercy."

Ques. What is the meaning of the Fifth Beatitude?

Ans. Jesus Christ teaches us that we ought not only not to steal what is not ours, but to give also of our own to those who are in want, that is, we should give alms.

Ques. Of how many kinds are works of charity?

Ans. Two: bodily and spiritual.

Ques. What are the bodily works of charity?

Ans. To feed the hungry, to clothe the naked, to visit the sick and prisoners, to receive willingly and to entertain strangers, to bury the dead poor, and generally never to do evil to a neighbor, but always good.

Ques. What are the spiritual works of charity?

Ans. By counsel to set the sinner free from his sin, and to bring him back into the way of salvation: to teach the ignorant the law of God, to give saving counsel to one's neighbor, when he is in danger or difficulty to pray to God for him, and to comfort those who are in trouble and sorrow.

The Sixth Beatitude

"Blessed are the pure in heart: for they shall see God."

Ques. What is the meaning of the Sixth Beatitude?

Ans. Since in the heart are born evil desires, and from evil desires are born evil acts, Jesus Christ calls blessed those who have cleansed their hearts from evil desires, for they shall see God.

The Seventh Beatitude

"Blessed are the peacemakers: for thay shall be called sons of God."

Ques. What is the meaning of the Seventh Beatitude?

Ans. Slander, evil speaking, strife, offences, envy, hatred and war are works of Satan, whilst peace is the work of God. Wherefore our Savior blesses the peacemakers, for they shall be called sons of God.

The Eighth Beatitude

"Blessed are they that are persecuted for righteousness' sake: for theirs is the Kingdom of Heaven."

Ques. What is the meaning of the Eighth Beatitude?

Ans. Jesus Christ blesses not the unjust, who persecute, but those who are unjustly treated and persecuted, for they shall be justified in the Kingdom of Heaven.

The Ninth Beatitude

"Blessed are ye, when men shall revile you, and persecute you, and shall say all manner of evil against you falsely, for My sake, Rejoice, and be exceedingly glad: for great is your reward in Heaven."

Ques. What is the meaning of the Ninth Beatitude?

Ans. The disciples and followers of Christ not only shall be wronged and persecuted, but shall be reviled and be evil spoken of, and shall endure all kinds of insults and mockery, and lying charges for the sake of Jesus Christ. But this is the greatest happiness and blessedness of any Christian who is thought worthy to suffer these things for Christ's sake. Joy and great gladness is his, because he has reached the highest step of Christian perfection, and great shall be his reward in the Kingdom of Heaven.

THE CHURCH OF HAGHIA SOPHIA
Constantinople.

SUPPLEMENT BY
CONSTANTINE CAVARNOS

The Theotokos as Hodegetria (Guide)
and the Child Christ
XIIth century mosaic,
Monastery of St. Catherine, Mount Sinai.

ORTHODOX ARCHITECTURE AND ICONOGRAPHY

Traditional Orthodox iconography, known as Byzantine, is a sacred, spiritual, anagogic art. Other major sacred arts of the Orthodox Church are Byzantine architecture, hymnography, and music. Iconography is best understood and appreciated when viewed in its relationship with these arts, and seen inside a Byzantine style church with the traditional Byzantine type iconostasis and several proskynetária (icon stands.)

"The form of the holy church building," according to Saint Symeon, Archbishop of Thessaloniki (died *c.* 1430), "represents the things that exist on earth, the things that exist in Heaven, and the things that exist above Heaven. The narthex represents the things on earth; the nave, Heaven; the most Holy Bema, the things that exist above Heaven."[1] [Facing eastward, the church is divided transversely from

[1] Symeon, Archbishop of Thessaloniki, Τὰ Ἅπαντα, ("All the Works"), Thessaloniki, *c.* 1960, p. 317.

the western towards the eastern end into the narthex (or outer and inner narthex), the nave, and the Holy Bema ("Sanctuary").] Amplifying this, Leonid Ouspensky (1902-1988), eminent Russian iconologist and iconographer, says that the narthex represents the earth, the unredeemed part of the world, and is for the penitents and the catechumens; the nave represents the created world justified, sanctified, deified, and is for the faithful laity; the Holy Bema, which is reserved for the clergy—bishops, priests, deacons—represents the Heaven of Heavens. [1] Symbolizing these levels, the floor of the nave is higher than that of the narthex, and the floor of the Holy Bema is higher than that of the nave.

A partition, called the *iconostasis* or *templon* and having mounted on it a varying number of panel icons, separates the nave from the Holy Bema.

Proskynetária—on which icons are set for veneration by the congregation—are placed in the nave.

The church, especially if domed, is so designed that its interior wall surfaces provide areas that are admirably suited for iconographic decoration. Also,

[1] Leonid Ouspensky, *Theology of the Icon*, New York, 1978, pp. 29-30.

it is built with materials and is given forms that endue it with good acoustic qualities, enabling the congregation to hear distinctly the sermons and hymns.

With regard to the domed church, it should be remarked that the prevailing form in Greece since the eleventh century has been the type known as the "cross-in-square." The ground plan of this church is rectangular, but its upper structure forms a cross. The ceiling of the nave is in the form of four barrel vaults that constitute the arms of a cross, intersecting at the dome. One of the barrel vaults is at the east end of the nave, one at the west end, and the other two at the north and south sides. On these four vaults and on the walls that support them are depicted events from the life of Christ and of the Theotokos, as well as various Saints.

Icons are distinguished, on the basis of their subject matter, into the *doctrinal*, the *festal*, and the *liturgical*. In the mural decoration of the church, each of these three types occupies a particular part of the edifice. Thus they constitute what Byzantinists call the *Doctrinal Cycle* (*Dogmatikós Kyklos*), the *Liturgical Cycle (Leitourgikós Kyklos)*, and the *Festal Cycle (Heortastikós Kyklos)*.

The Main Church of the Monastery of Lavra on Mount Athos.
View from the northeast

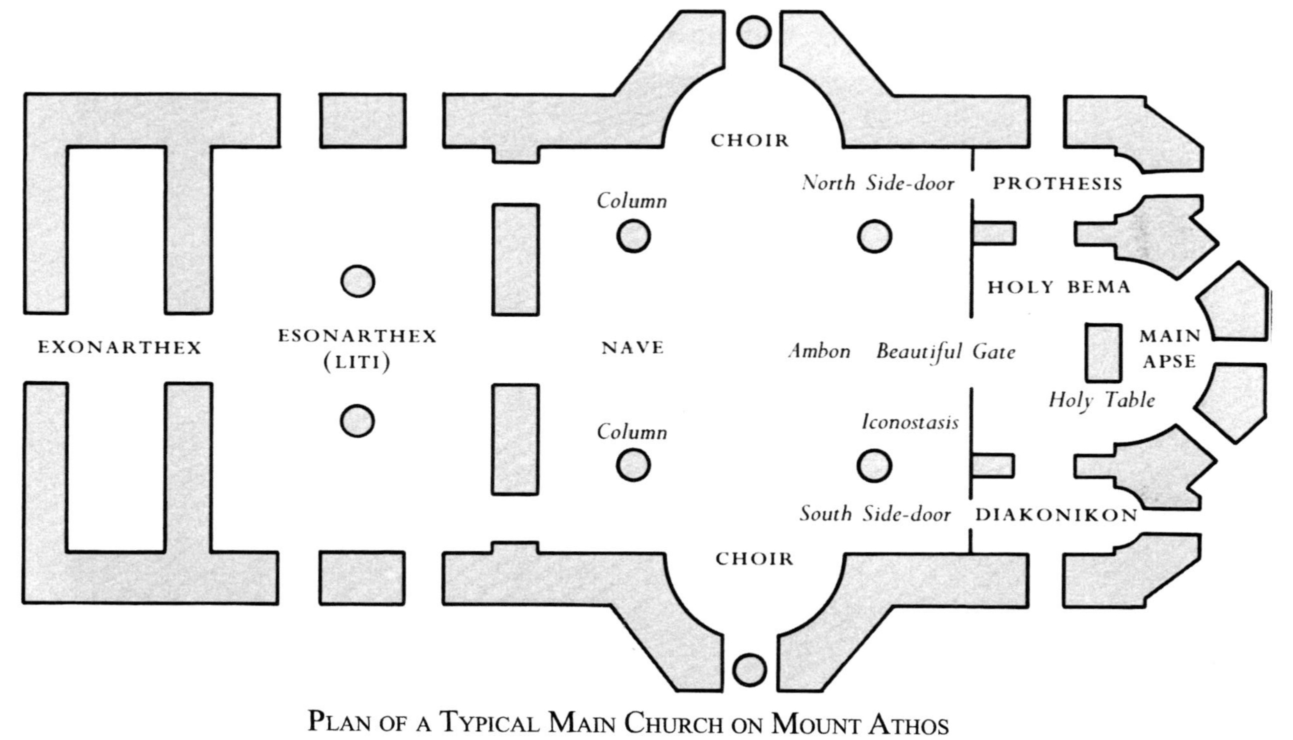

PLAN OF A TYPICAL MAIN CHURCH ON MOUNT ATHOS

BASILICA OF ST. DEMETRIOS AT THESSALONIKI
Vth century domeless basilica as restored after the fire of 1917.

Church of St. Demetrios
The interior as restored.

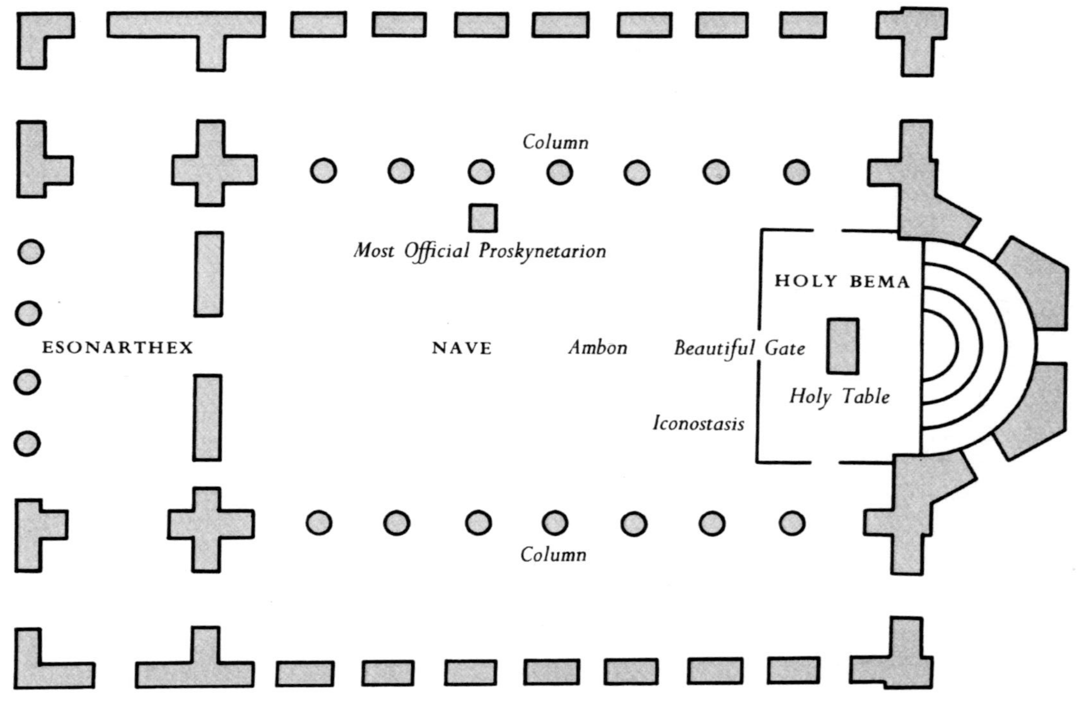

Ground Plan of a Typical Byzantine Domeless Basilica

THE ICONOSTASIS

The origin of the iconostasis can be traced back to the Old Testament period, for we read in one of its books, the *Exodus*, that a "curtain" or "veil," called in the *Septuagint* version the *katapétasma*, was used to separate the holy place (*to hágion)* and the holy of holies (*to hágion ton hagíon)*. The curtain had the figures of Cherubim on it and was hung on four wooden pillars *(styloi)* overlaid with gold. This was done in accordance with the following order that was given by God to Moses: "And thou shalt make a veil of dark blue, and purple, and scarlet, and fine twined linen, a woven work, with Cherubim. And thou shalt set it upon four posts of incorruptible wood overlaid with gold.... And the veil shall make a separation between the holy and the holy of holies" (Exodus 26:31-33).

The distinguished Byzantinist George Soteriou (1880-1965) has this to say about the iconostasis:

"Panel icons were placed on the *Iconostásion* or *Templon* especially after the period of Iconoclasm [i.e., after 843]. The *Iconostásion* was divided into

PROSKYNETARION AND CANDLE STAND
In the nave of a church in Lesvos. 1779.

A TRADITIONAL ICONOSTASIS
Chapel of the Monastery of Barlaam, Meteora.

two parts, the lower and the upper. The lower part had between its three doors the large icons of the chiefest holy personages of the Christian religion: Christ, the Theotokos, and John the Forerunner, and also the icon of the Saint to whom the church was dedicated.... At the upper part were placed, in chronological sequence, and in accordance with the calendar of holy days of the Church, small icons of the cycle of holy days pertaining to Christ and the Theotokos."[1]

Like Soteriou, David Talbot Rice (1903-1972), eminent British historian of Byzantine art, holds that the iconostasis "developed in the Byzantine world." He says that "indeed, it is hardly possible to think of a Byzantine interior without wall-paintings and iconostasis, for the painted picture was a very essential feature in the Liturgy, and the iconostasis was in fact a frame on to which additional pictures [i.e., icons] could be attached." Rice goes on to add that in early times the iconostasis "was comparatively modest in size, but by the twelfth century wood had generally replaced stone [i.e., marble],

[1] Τὸ Ἅγιον Ὄρος, Athens, 1915, pp. 128-129.

and the iconostasis had been increased considerably in height."[1] He remarks, further, that from that time tier above tier of panel icons was affixed to it. When he makes this statement, he has in mind what happened in Russia; for in Byzantium and in post-Byzantine Greece the number of tiers did not grow to three or more, as it did among the Russians.

The iconostasis is pierced at the middle by a large doorway, called the *Beautiful Gate (Horaía Pyle)*—a term taken from the New Testament (*Acts of the Apostles* 3:2, 10)—and two smaller doorways, one near the north (left) end of the iconostasis and one near its south (right) end.

Of the lower-tier icons, the two most official ones, called "Sovereign" *(Despotikaí)*, are placed immediately next to the Beautiful Gate: to the south of it the icon of Christ, to the north of it that of the Theotokos with the Child. Traditionally and properly, they are busts, not full-figure depictions. They are half-figures for greater spiritual expressiveness. For the face, the most expressive part of the body,

[1] *Byzantine Art*, revised edition, London and Baltimore, 1962, p.74.

can be depicted in such a painting in much larger dimensions and thus be rendered more clearly visible to the congregation than in full-figure.

Next to the icon of Christ is placed that of Saint John the Baptist, either bust or full-length figure; and next to that of the Theotokos, the holy person, persons, or event specially commemorated by the church. When there is only one such person, he is preferably shown half-figure; when there are two or more persons, they are depicted full-figure. (In some churches the icon of the Baptist has been set next to the icon of the Theotokos, and that of the person(s) or event specially celebrated by the church has been placed next to that of Christ.) If space permits, additional icons are placed on the lower tier.

The greatest emphasis is given to the two "Sovereign" icons through the *centrality* of the position they occupy. The principle of psychological perspective is obviously applied in so placing them. The same principle is applied in having the Theotokos holding the Child Christ on her left side, thereby bringing Him closer to the center, to the Beautiful Gate.

At its lower half, the Beautiful Gate has a set of folding doors, called *Bemóthyra* ("doors of the Bema"). They are closed at certain points of the Divine Liturgy and other offices, and remain closed when there is no service. They also serve as panels for the art of iconography. Usually, the Annunciation is depicted on them: the Archangel Gabriel on the north wing and the Theotokos on the south wing. Sometimes, there are added the figures of the Prophet-kings David and Solomon, and those of the Apostles Peter and Paul, or the four Evangelists: Matthew, John, Mark and Luke, or four Hierarchs. The Annunciation in such cases occupies the upper half of the *Bemóthyra*, with the two Prophet-kings at either end of it, while the other figures occupy the lower half of it.

On the side doors of the iconostasis are depicted the Archangels Michael (on the north door) and Gabriel (on the south door). Sometimes Saints George and Demetrios are painted instead. Only the upper half of the door is utilized for them, and only the upper half of the body is shown. The representation of them in full figure occupying the whole door, which is seen in many churches that have been decorated in recent times, is an unwarranted deviation from tradition. It gives them undue emphasis, since their full-figure representation is twice the size of that of Christ and the Theotokos, who are the most important personages shown on the iconostasis.

The iconostasis' second tier of icons comprises small icons either of the Twelve Great Festivals, called in Greek the *Dodekáorton*, or of the Twelve Apostles in the form of a *Megále Déesis*, "Great Supplication."

THEOLOGY OF HOLY ICONS[1]

The Decrees (Πράξεις) of the Seventh Holy, Great Oecumenical Synod state the following with regard to the making and use of holy icons:

This Holy and Oecumenical Synod has assembled in this glorious metropolis of Nicaea for the second time [in 787], having by reading understood the doctrines of our venerable and blessed Fathers, glorifies God Himself, by Whom wisdom was given to them for our instruction and for the formation of the Universal *(Katholiké)* and Apostolic Church. Those, however, who do not accept these doctrines but contrive to obscure the real truth by their own innovations *(kainotomíai)*, are subdued with the Psalmist's voice: "The enemies have done

[1] I have made the translation of these excerpts from the ancient Greek text contained in Mansi's *Sacrorum Conciliorum Nova et Amplissima Collectio*, Florence, 1767, Vol. 13, cols. 129, 132, 377, 380.

wickedly in Thy holy places! And they have boasted, saying that 'There is no more any teacher, and there is none who will know that we distorted the word of truth.'"[1] But we, keeping in every respect the doctrines and ordinances of our God-inspired Fathers, proclaim with one mouth and one heart, neither adding anything to nor taking anything from that which has been transmitted to us by them; but these we stoutly affirm, by these we stand fast. Thus we confess, thus we teach, as the six Holy and Oecumenical Synods have defined and established....

We salute *(aspazómetha)*[2] the form of the venerable and life-giving Cross, and the holy relics of the saints, and we receive, salute, and kiss the holy and venerable icons, according to the ancient tradition of the holy Universal Church of God, and of our holy Fathers, *who both received them and determined that they should be in all the most holy churches of God*, and in every place of His Dominion. To these holy and venerable icons, as we have

[1] Psalm 73:3-4, 9 (Septuagint).

[2] 'Saluting' an icon consists in performing such acts as bowing before it, crossing oneself, saying a prayer, and kissing it.

said, we give honor *(timomen)* and salutation and *honorable reverence (timetikós proskynoúmen)*: namely, the *icon* of the *Incarnation* of our great God and Savior *Jesus Christ*, and of our immaculate Lady and all-holy *Theotokos*, of whom He was pleased to become incarnate, that He might save us and deliver us from every impious madness after idols; also of the incorporeal *Angels* – since they appeared to the righteous in the form of men. Also the forms and icons of the divine and most famed *Apostles*, of the *Prophets*, who speak of God, of the victorious *Martyrs*, and of *other Saints; in order that by their paintings we may be enabled to rise to the remembrance and memory of the prototype, and may partake in some measure of sanctification.* These things we have been taught to hold, and have been confirmed in holding, by our holy Fathers and their divinely delivered teachings....

We keep all the ecclesiastical traditions which have been handed down to us, whether written, or unwritten, free of innovations. One of the traditions which we thus preserve is that of *making representational paintings, which is in accord with the history of the preaching of the Gospel, as confirming the real and not merely the imaginary incarnation of God the Logos,* [1] *and as contributing to our good in other ways.* For those things which illustrate each other emphasize each other.

These things being so, we, as proceeding in the royal pathway, and following the divinely inspired teaching of our holy Fathers, and the Tradition of the Universal Church—for we know that it is of the Holy Spirit which dwells in her—define with all exactness and care that just as the form (*typos*) of the precious and life-giving Cross, so also the venerable and holy icons, *both in painting and mosaic and other fit materials,* [2] should be set forth in the

[1] The representation of Christ is of special theological significance, as an affirmation of His Incarnation. To reject Christ's icon is virtually to deny His Incarnation; to accept and venerate it is to affirm and recall His Incarnation.

[2] In the Western Church, extensive use has been made of stained glass, so it was obviously assumed in the West that this is fit material for depicting sacred persons and events. But in the East, in the Orthodox Church, stained glass has not been used in iconographic decoration. Orthodox iconographers have regarded it as unsuitable, or at any rate far inferior to the mosaic and the fresco, which they have used for the representation of sacred figures on

holy churches of God, on the sacred vessels and vestments, and on walls and panels of wood, both in houses and by the roads—that is, the icon of our Lord God and Savior *Jesus Christ*, of our spotless Lady the *Theotokos*, of the honorable *Angels*, and of *all Saints and Holy Men. For the more continually they are seen in iconic form, the more are the beholders lifted up to the memory of the prototypes and to an aspiration after them.*

To these should be given *salutation (aspasmós) and honorable reverence (timetiké proskynesis), not* indeed the *true worship (latreía) of faith, which pertains to the divine nature alone.* But in the same way as to the form of the precious and life-giving

the walls, domes, vaults, apses and arches. One consideration was probably the fact that icons made of stained glass, when compared with frescoes, mosaics, and panels, seem crude works, with broken up bodies, whose diverse fragments are held together by unaesthetic pieces of metal. Another important consideration was probably the fact that icons made of stained glass are non-functional during night services, when there is no light outside to illuminate them. The whole window on which the figures are depicted is then just a solid piece of blackness. It is otherwise with frescoes, mosaics, and panel icons: even the dim illumination provided by the candles and oil-burning sacred lamps renders their forms and colors visible.

Cross and to the holy Book of the Gospels and to the rest of the sacred objects, so to these also shall be offered *incense and lights*,[1] in honor of them, according to the ancient pious custom. *For the honor which is paid to the icon passes on to that which the icon represents, and he who reveres the icon reveres in it the person who is represented.* For thus the teaching of our holy Fathers, that is, the tradition of the Universal Church, which from one end of the earth to the other has received the Gospel, is strengthened. Thus we follow Paul, who spoke in Christ, and the entire divine Apostolic company and the holy Fathers, holding the traditions which we have received.

[1] To this day lights are offered by the Orthodox in honor of icons, both in the church and at home. In the church, a sacred lamp *(kandéli)* is suspended before each of the large icons on the lower part of the iconostasis, as well as before certain others, while at home there is an ever-burning sacred lamp placed in front of the icons that are set on a small icon stand in one of the rooms.

HYMNODY OF THE CHURCH

Orthodox hymnody is one of the most precious treasures of the Church. This hymnody is distinguished into two kinds, the liturgical and the merely religious. Of these, the first is the more important. Liturgical hymnody consists of hymns that are intended to be chanted in church, and is employed in all the services. The poetry here conforms to sacred melodies. The merely religious hymns, on the other hand, are intended simply to be read. Both of these kinds of poetry are original in form as well as in content. St. Romanos the Melodist and St. John of Damascus are the greatest composers of liturgical hymns, while St. Gregory Nazianzen and St. Symeon the New Theologian are among the most important writers of non-liturgical hymns. There have been numerous other hymnographers whose works are of great merit, both as poetry and as theology or "sacred philosophy."

We shall concern ourselves here with the liturgical hymnody alone. This is contained in six liturgical collections making up seventeen large volumes: the *Parakletiké* or *Great Octóechos*, the *Triódion*, the *Pentekostárion*, the *Menaía*, the *Great Horológion*, and the *Great Evchológion*.

The *Parakletiké* contains chiefly hymns commemorating the Resurrection of Christ, together with canons addressed to the Holy Trinity. The canon is the most elaborate type of hymn, generally consisting of eight odes, and sometimes of nine.

In the *Triodión* are included the services for the Great Lent and the four weeks that precede it. The hymns of this book have reference to various events in the Old and the New Testaments, but especially to the Passion of Jesus.

The *Pentekostárion* contains the Pascha service and the services for all the subsequent movable holy days until the Sunday of All Saints – the Sunday after Pentecost.

The *Menaia* are twelve volumes, one for each month of the year. In the Eastern Church, each day of the month has a special vesper service (*hesperinós*) and matins (*órthros*), containing hymns for the saint or saints commemorated on that day; and hence each volume of this collection is divided into as many parts as the particular month for which it has been composed has days.

In the *Great Horológion* are contained chiefly the *apolytíkia* and *kontákia* for all the holy days of the year, and certain *akolouthias* or services such as the *Akáthistos Hymn*, the canons of entreaty to the Theotokos or Holy Virgin Mary, etc. An *apolytíkion* is a short laudatory hymn that is chanted at Vespers, the Orthros, and the Divine Liturgy, and has reference to the holy person or event commemorated on the particular day when it is chanted, while a *kontákion* is a short hymn which sums up the significance of the life of a saint or expresses the main point of the occasion for which it is used. The *Akáthistos Hymn* is a special *akolouthia*, dating from the 6th century, dedicated to the Theotokos and held on the first five Fridays of the Great Lent.

Finally, the *Great Evchológion*, "Great Prayer Book," comprises the liturgies of St. Chrysostom and St. Basil, the services for the seven Mysteria, and prayers for various occasions.

The language in which Byzantine liturgical hymns are written is the ancient Greek, although often in a fairly simplified form. However, this poetry owes little to classical models. What it has in common with the latter, besides the Greek language, is chiefly clarity, simplicity, and restraint—qualities that characterize classical Greek genius. These hymns are distinguished by *free rhythm* and, generally, by a *lack of rhyme*. Measured rhythm or meter, which Westerners expect to find in hymns, is not to be found in these. Rhyme is employed only occasionally, particularly for the purpose of emphasizing a connection between certain thoughts. The form of the language of these hymns can best be characterized as *cadenced poetic prose*. There are exceptions, such as certain hymns of St. John Damascene, which are in iambics.

The *inner essence* of Byzantine hymnody is identical with that of Byzantine music, architecture, and iconography. Hymnody differs from them only in employing a different medium: language. Like them it seeks to introduce us to a realm of being that lies beyond the world which is apprehended by the senses, to lift us to a higher level of experience, to the level of spiritual beauty, of holiness, of the Divine.

The themes of the hymnographer are the Holy Trinity, Christ, the Theotokos, the Prophets, the

Apostles, the Martyrs, the Church Fathers and the rest of the Saints, and in some instances the Archangels. They are the power, wisdom, justice, mercy, beauty and other attributes of God; the life, teaching, and miracles of Christ; the life and virtues of the Theotokos and of the Saints. These themes are treated *objectively*, without the poet injecting into them either his idiosyncrasy or matters pertaining to his own individual life. This point is brought out with great clarity and emphasis by John Brownlie in his book *Hymns of the Greek Church*. "One prime characteristic of Greek hymnody," he remarks, "should be referred to. Unlike our English hymn which is intensely subjective—in many cases unhealthily so—the Greek hymn is in most cases objective. God, in the glory of His majesty, and clothed with His attributes, is held up to the worship and adoration of His people. Christ in His person and work is set before the mind in a most realistic manner. His birth and its accompaniments; His life; the words He spoke and the works He did; His passion in all the agony of its detail; the denial of Peter; the remorse of Judas; the Crucifixion; the darkness, the terror, the opened graves; the penitent thief, the loud cry, the death; — all are depicted in plain unmistakable language. So we have in the hymns of the Greek Church a pictorial representation of the history of Redemption which, by engaging the mind, appeals ultimately to the heart and its emotions."[1]

It is not his ego or his place and time that the hymnographer seeks to express, but the facts, truths, and values of Christian religion, and the feelings that it is proper for a devout Christian to express, such as praise of God and of the Saints, gratitude to them, entreaty, hope and love.

Thus, the following Resurrectional Apolytikion of the Fourth Mode expresses the event described in Luke 24:1-10:

"The women disciples of the Lord, having learned from the Angel the joyous proclamation of the Resurrection, and the abolition of the ancestral sentence, with exultation announced to the Apostles: Death is despoiled, Christ our God has risen, and gives to the world the Great Mercy."

The Resurrectional Apolytikion of the First Plagal Mode is a hymn of praise to Christ:

[1] *Op. cit.*, Paisley, 1902.

"Let us, the faithful, praise and worship the Logos, co-eternal with the Father and the Spirit, and for our salvation born of a Virgin; for He willed to be lifted upon the Cross in the flesh, and to endure death, and to raise the dead by His glorious Resurrection."

Feelings of praise are also conveyed by the following *Martyrikon*, or hymn addressed to the Martyrs:

"Let all peoples honor with hymns and spiritual odes the Victorious Martyrs of Christ, the luminaries of the world and heralds of the Faith, the eternal fount from which there gush up cures for the faithful."

Often such hymns end as exhortations to the faithful to imitate the Martyrs' virtues and deeds.

In the following hymn, which is chanted on Pascha, the feeling of hope finds vivid expression:

"Oh, how divine, how beloved, how superlatively sweet is Thy voice! Because Thou hast promised us, O Christ, that Thou wilt be with us until the end of time. And we, holding onto Thy words as to an anchor of hope, are glad and rejoice."

Frequently, hymns are entreaties addressed to God asking for aid whereby the faithful may overcome temptations, become truthful, courageous, meek, blameless, pure, sharers of God's wisdom and blessedness. The following hymn, which is chanted in the *Orthros* of the Sunday of the Publican and the Pharisee, is an example:

"O Thou Giver-of-life, open for me the gates of repentance; for my spirit, entirely defiled, bearing the temple of the body, chants the morning office before Thy temple. But Thou, being merciful, cleanse me through Thy compassionate mercy." [8]

Hymns of entreaty are often addressed to the Theotokos, the Apostles, and other Saints, as intercessors with God. It is a belief, deeply rooted in the Orthodox consciousness, that the Saints, who when on earth prayed for their brethren, continue to intercede for them with the Lord after their death, as members of the triumphant Church of Christ in Heaven. This belief finds vivid expression in Orthodox hymnody. Thus, the hymn that immediately follows the one just quoted is addressed to the Theotokos and says:

"Make straight for me the paths of salvation, O Theotokos; for I have defiled my soul with ugly sins, having spent my whole life in a state of inner sleep. Through thy intercessions deliver me from every impurity."

The same type of entreaty is expressed in the following hymn to the Apostles:

"Apostles who have seen God, illumine my soul, which is darkened by passions—you who through your divine teachings have illumined the world and diminished the darkness of the idols. And now intercede that peace and the Great Mercy be given to our souls."

The concern for the beautiful is of the essence of Byzantine hymnody. But the beauty that concerns it is the spiritual, not the physical. The latter is brought into the hymns only by way of comparison as a means of expressing the beauty that is spiritual. Hymns are often adorned with words denoting beauty—*kállos, horaiótes, horaíos, kalloné*—indicating spiritual beauty. The concern is for the beauty of the Holy Trinity, of the Divine Logos—Christ—of the mind, of the soul, of the virtues. At every opportunity the hymnographers extol the beauty of God, of the uncreated Divine Light, of the blessed Angels and Saints, who mirror divine Beauty by their possession of piety, purity, love, and other beautiful qualities. They seek thereby not only to praise God and His holy followers in a worthy manner, but also to arouse the worshippers spiritually, to incite them to apply themselves with greater energy to the urgent task of transforming their inner being. Characteristic in this regard are the following hymns, in which God is viewed as the supreme, ineffable Beauty that is the ultimate source of beauty of the soul:

"Thou wast transfigured on the Mountain, O Christ our God, having shown to Thy disciples Thy glory as they were able to behold it. Shine upon us sinners, too, Thy light eternal, through the intercessions of the Theotokos. O Giver-of-light, glory to Thee."

"Thou hast created the incorporeal and heavenly Angelic Hosts as mirrors of Thy beauty, O indivisible Trinity, Sole Ruler, to sing unceasingly to Thee. And now accept from our earthen lips our hymn of praise."

"Make straight the hearts of Thy servants towards the unapproachable Light, O Thrice resplendent Lord, and bestow the effulgence of Thy glory upon our souls that we may behold Thy ineffable beauty."

GENERAL INDEX